Father Sun and Mother Earth Create Life

Creator and illustrator: Patrick Arguin

English translation: Bleu Dactylo

French version written by: Michèle Rappe
Support, coaching and collaboration: Hélène Beaudette

I want to offer my deepest gratitude to Hélène Beaudette.
Her unconditional support and presence allowed TOOLS OF THE HEART to grow and come into form.

Once upon a time, living among the stars, there was a beautiful blue planet called Earth. Nearby was a very big and bright star called the Sun.

The Sun was warm and comforting. The Earth was carrying a lot of water, which was covering most of her surface.

Every day they would spend a lot of time together.

As time passed by, they loved each other more and more every day. So they decided to grow a garden together.

They would come up with plenty of ideas for their garden and even found a name for it. They would call it *Life*!

The Earth then decided to share an important secret with the Sun; «I discovered that there is a rainbow of wisdom in everyone's heart,» she said.

The Sun was deeply moved and overjoyed. Together, they kept planning and dreaming about their garden. The Earth would carry Life, while the Sun would cuddle her with love and support.

The Sun began to warm the Earth with greater energy, making the waters slowly evaporate. Sometimes, clouds would gather in the sky, and it would rain for days, but the soft warmth of the Sun would always return. The blue planet was changing, revealing more and more land.

At last, one day, the garden began to grow.

The Earth and the Sun were excited. They were finally a mom and a dad! They were beaming with love.

However, one morning, their garden did not look so well.
Worried, they asked a dear friend for help.

The Moon reassured her friends.

«By learning to breathe deeply, Mother Earth will allow the garden to bloom and flourish,» she said. «But how?» asked Mother Earth and Father Sun.

The Moon smiled and asked,
«Dear Earth, did you forget about
your rainbow of wisdom?»

Mother Earth closed her eyes to feel what was deep within her heart. She felt a soothing sensation, and her wisdom popped up, looking like a red elf.

Red guided the Earth how to breathe gently and deeply. He explained to her that when breathing in, she would feel her belly go out. Then, by breathing out, she would feel her belly go in.

By breathing this way and finding her rhythm, Mother Earth felt calmed and relaxed.

She felt so good after that; she wanted to share this discovery with everyone!

She talked to the garden about the rainbow of wisdom. She then explained how to go in one's heart to meet the red elf, who knows how to breathe in and out slowly and deeply.

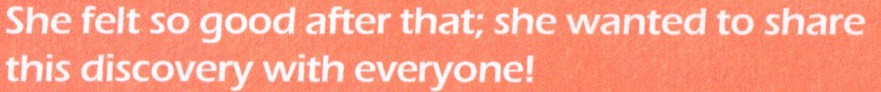

Together, they learned how to breathe this way.

Inhale. Hmffffff...
Exhale. Pffffffffff...

Inhale. Hmffffff...
Exhale. Pffffffffff...

Inhale. Hmffffff...
Exhale. Pffffffffff...

Everyone in the garden now knows about their rainbow of wisdom. When they feel the need to, they stop for a moment.

They close their eyes and breathe slowly and deeply to feel better, just like the red elf taught them.

High in the sky, stars celebrate with Father Sun and Mother Earth who embrace their garden with love.

Together, they continue to teach everyone in the garden how to breathe slowly and deeply.

As for the moon...
She is still there, happily gazing upon the sleeping garden.
She takes comfort in knowing that a heart full of love is an
extraordinary gift for life!

Remember...

How do I breathe in and out like Mother Earth?

Close your eyes and put one hand on your heart. Put the other hand on your belly. Inhale through your nose and exhale slowly. Feel your belly going in and out.
Repeat three times.

Why is it important to breathe deeply like that?

If you need a moment, breathing slowly and deeply will help your body to relax and feel energized again. This little moment of calmness can help you to find your rhythm and enjoy the rest of the day!

What if I'm too excited or fidgety?

When you take the time to breathe slowly and deeply, it helps you find your calm and your well-being, even if you feel too excited or fidgety.

The Book Collection

Tools of the Heart
Fostering Confidence and Self-esteem

1 Father Sun and Mother Earth Create Life
Breathing/Finding your rhythm

Breathing is essential to life; conscious breathing is a simple, yet effective way to regain your calm and well-being by finding your body's rhythm.

2 Fluffy and the Rainbow in his Heart
Meditation/Finding your inner calm

Each one of us has a peaceful place inside their heart. Meditation is a tool that allows you to find your personal space or to go back to it.

3 Colin Discovers Confidence
Grounding/Strengthening your self-confidence

Growing up often comes with its share of fears and hesitations. Growing solid roots helps to build and nurture a positive self-confidence.

4 Colin and Fluffy Become Friends
Knowing yourself/Loving and appreciating

Positive self-confidence and self-esteem are the building blocks of healthy relationships; therefore, learning to appreciate who we are is a treasure for life.

5 The Choice
Insight/Listening to your intuition

Learning to listen to your inner voice and how to trust it, is learning to stay true to yourself in all situations.

6 Colin's Courage
Expressing/Confidence in yourself

Standing up for yourself is not wrong. It is about relying on your self-worth with confidence, to respectfully say what you need to say.

7 Enough is Enough
Self-respect/Daring to be yourself

Developing good communication skills also implies expressing your feelings and needs in a respectful manner, which can sometimes be a challenge!

8 Fluffy Finds his Well-being
Self-awareness/Taking responsibility

Growing up is also about becoming more aware of your emotions and learning to manage them responsibly.

The Meditation Collection

Tools of the Heart
Fostering Confidence and Self-esteem

Specially designed for young children, the guided meditations explore and develop the same themes, as seen in the **Tools of the Heart** book collection. These intend to reinforce the children's knowledge of themselves through their inner space of wisdom, where things can be seen, heard, and felt.

Meditation is also a wonderful tool that children can easily learn to help them self-regulate physically, mentally, and emotionally.

To learn more, go to our website:
www.toolsoftheheart.com